THE GRAPHIC
SHAKESPEARE SERIES

JULIUS CAESAR

Published by
Evans Brothers Limited
2A Portman Mansions
Chiltern Street
London W1M 1LE

© in the modern text Hilary Burningham 1997
© in the illustrations Evans Brothers Ltd 1997
Designed by Design Systems Ltd.

British Library Cataloguing in Publication Data
Burningham, Hilary
    Julius Caesar. – (The graphic Shakespeare series)
    1. Children's plays, English
    I. Title II. May, Dan III. Shakespeare, William, 1564-1616
    822.3'3

ISBN 0 237 51783 3

Printed in Hong Kong by Wing King Tong Co. Ltd.

THE GRAPHIC
SHAKESPEARE SERIES

JULIUS CAESAR

RETOLD BY HILARY BURNINGHAM
ILLUSTRATED BY DAN MAY

EVANS BROTHERS LIMITED

THE CHARACTERS IN THE PLAY

Julius Caesar: – ruler of Rome

Calphurnia: – wife of Caesar

Mark Antony: – friend of Caesar
member of Triumvirate

Cassius: – the first conspirator

Marcus Brutus: – a powerful man, friend of Caesar,
joined the conspiracy

Portia: – wife of Brutus

Lucius: – servant to Brutus

Other conspirators were:

Casca

Cinna

Decius Brutus

Metellus Cimber

Flavius:
Marullus: } – tribunes

The Soothsayer: – person who can see into the future

Artemidorus: – a teacher

Octavius Caesar: – Caesar's nephew and adopted son,
member of Triumvirate

Lepidus: – third member of Triumvirate

Titinius:
Messala: } – fought on the side of Brutus and
Cassius at Philippi

Strato: } – Brutus's servant
Pindarus: } – Cassius's servant

PORTRAIT GALLERY

Julius Caesar

Calphurnia

Brutus

Portia

Cassius

Mark Anthony

Casca

Cinna

Decius

Octavius

Flavius

Marullus

Soothsayer

Artemidorus

ACT 1

It was the Roman Feast of Lupercal. The Feast of Lupercal was a religious day; it was not a holiday.

Flavius and Marullus were tribunes (important men in Rome). They met a group of workmen all dressed in their best clothes.

The tribunes asked the workmen why they were dressed in their best clothes on a working day.

The workmen said they were having a holiday to celebrate Caesar's victory.

Flavius and Marullus were very angry. They were angry because Caesar had fought Pompey, a noble Roman. Before, the people had cheered for Pompey; now they cheered for Caesar.

Flavius and Marullus shouted at the workmen and told them to go home.

MARULLUS: And do you now put on your best attire?
And do you now cull out a holiday?
And do you now strew flowers in his way
That comes in triumph over Pompey's blood?
Be gone!

Julius Caesar

People had decorated the statues of Caesar. Flavius and Marullus decided to pull the decorations down. Caesar was getting too powerful!

FLAVIUS: Disrobe the images,
           If you do find them decked with ceremonies.
MARULLUS: May we do so?
           You know it is the feast of Lupercal.
FLAVIUS: It is no matter; let no images
           Be hung with Caesar's trophies.

Caesar walked through the streets. A soothsayer[1] called out to him, "Beware the ides of March!"[2]

[1]soothsayer – a person who tells what is going to happen in the future.
[2]the ides of March – the fifteenth of March; a special day.

CAESAR:	Who is it in the press that calls on me? I hear a tongue shriller than all the music Cry 'Caesar!' Speak. Caesar is turned to hear.
SOOTHSAYER:	Beware the ides of March.
CAESAR:	What man is that?
BRUTUS:	A soothsayer bids you beware the ides of March.

Cassius had a long talk with Brutus. Brutus admitted that he was worried. The Romans had always been very proud that the power of the government was shared among many people. Now, Caesar was becoming too powerful. Brutus did not want one man to have all the power.

Cassius and Brutus could hear the people shouting. Were they asking Caesar to be their king?

Cassius told Brutus two stories. First, how he once saved Caesar from drowning. Second, how Caesar had been ill with a fever and cried for water. There were times when Caesar was weak and feeble. Now, he had power over them all.

Brutus said he would think about how they could stop Caesar. Cassius was quite pleased.

BRUTUS: What means this shouting? I do fear the people
Choose Caesar for their king.
CASSIUS: Ay, do you fear it?
Then must I think you would not have it so.
BRUTUS: I would not, Cassius; yet I love him well.
But wherefore do you hold me here so long?
What is it that you would impart to me?

Caesar returned with his friends and supporters. He saw Brutus and Cassius talking together. He told his friend Mark Antony that Cassius was a dangerous man. Mark Antony told him not to worry.

CAESAR: Yond Cassius has a lean and hungry look;
He thinks too much: such men are dangerous.
ANTONY: Fear him not, Caesar; he's not dangerous;
He is a noble Roman, and well given.

Brutus and Cassius stopped Casca, and asked him what had happened in the market place.

Casca told them what he had seen. Mark Antony had three times offered Caesar a crown. Three times, Caesar had refused to take it.

It seemed to Casca that Caesar really wanted to take the crown. Casca, who did not like Caesar, said it was all a lot of nonsense.

Next, Caesar had fallen down.[1]

Marullus and Flavius were punished for taking the decorations off Caesar's statues.

Casca was disgusted at the way the crowd loved Caesar.

[1]Caesar had epilepsy – a condition that causes fainting. In Shakespeare's time it was called "the falling sickness" because people fainted and fell down.

CASCA: I saw Mark Antony offer him a crown; yet 'twas not a crown neither, 'twas one of these coronets; and, as I told you, he put it by once; but for all that, to my thinking, he would fain have had it.

Brutus, Casca and Cassius agreed to meet the next day. Brutus was a good man who loved his country. He and Caesar were friends. He had a lot to think about.

Cassius wanted Brutus to join him in a plot against Caesar. Everyone in Rome thought that Brutus was a good man.

Brutus would not want to kill Caesar, because he and Caesar were friends. Caesar trusted him.

Cassius knew how to persuade Brutus. He decided to write letters to Brutus, pretending that they came from other people. The letters would say that Caesar was getting too powerful, and Brutus should do something about it.

Cassius was willing to lie and cheat to get Brutus on his side. This showed he was not a good man.

CASSIUS: ...I will this night,
In several hands, in at his windows throw,
As if they came from several citizens,
Writings, all tending to the great opinion
That Rome holds of his name...
And after this, let Caesar seat him sure,
For we will shake him, or worse days endure.

It was night time. There was thunder and lightning.
Strange things were happening in Rome. A lion
walked the streets. A slave held up his hand. It
seemed to be on fire, yet his hand was not burnt.
There were many other strange sights.

All these things made people feel that something
terrible was going to happen.

CASCA: A common slave -- you know him well by sight --
Held up his left hand, which did flame and burn
Like twenty torches joined; and yet his hand,
...remained unscorched.

Cassius enjoyed the terrible night. He met Casca in the street and they talked about Caesar. Casca agreed that Caesar should be stopped.

This was the beginning of the plot to kill Caesar. The people in the plot were called conspirators[1]. The main conspirators were Cinna, Casca and Cassius.

They needed Brutus to join them because he was a very good man. He was also famous and the people admired him.

Cassius gave Cinna three fake letters he had written. Cinna was to put them where Brutus would find them.

[1]conspirators – a group of people secretly planning together.

CASSIUS: ...Good Cinna, take this paper,
And look you lay it in the praetor's chair,
Where Brutus may but find it; and throw this
In at his window; set this up with wax
Upon old Brutus' statue. All this done,
Repair to Pompey's porch, where you shall find us.

ACT 2

Brutus was in his garden. He had been thinking and worrying all night. What should he do about Caesar?

Caesar had become too powerful.

Brutus's servant, Lucius, had found a letter. It was one of the fake letters that Cassius had sent. It was supposed to come from an ordinary person, telling Brutus to act against Caesar. Brutus believed the letter came from a real person.

Lucius told him that the next day was the ides of March.

LUCIUS: ...I found
This paper, thus sealed up; and I am sure
It did not lie there when I went to bed.

The conspirators (the men planning to kill Caesar) came to see Brutus.

Cassius was their leader. The others were: Casca, Cinna, Decius Brutus, Metellus Cimber and Trebonius.

Brutus decided to join the conspirators, and shook hands with them. Cassius wanted all the conspirators to swear an oath[1] to carry out their plan. Brutus thought an oath was not a good idea. The conspirators did as Brutus wished. They did not swear an oath.

[1]oath – a solemn promise before God.

BRUTUS: ...What other bond
Than secret Romans that have spoke the word,
And will not palter? And what other oath
Than honesty to honesty engaged...?

Brutus and Cassius had a disagreement.

Should they kill only Caesar? Should they kill Mark Antony as well?

Cassius thought that Mark Antony, who loved Caesar, could be very dangerous to them.

Brutus thought that Mark Antony would be nothing without Caesar. He also thought that if they killed both men, they would seem to be "too bloody".

Cassius was not happy, but he had to give in to Brutus.

Brutus had his way. They agreed not to kill Mark Antony.

Next, they thought about the next day, the day they planned to murder Caesar. Terrible things had happened in the night. Cassius was worried that Caesar might not want to go out.

Decius Brutus said that he would persuade Caesar to go to the Capitol[1].

[1]the Capitol – the meeting place.

CASSIUS: ...I think it is not meet
               Mark Antony, so well beloved of Caesar,
               Should outlive Caesar. We shall find of him
               A shrewd contriver; ...
BRUTUS: Our course will seem too bloody, Caius Cassius,
               To cut the head off and then hack the limbs,
               Like wrath in death, and envy afterwards;
               For Antony is but a limb of Caesar.

Portia, Brutus's wife, came to him in the orchard. She was very worried about him. She knew he had something on his mind. She had seen the conspirators, and noticed that they hid their faces from her. On her knees, she asked Brutus to tell her what was going on.

Brutus promised to tell Portia everything later.

BRUTUS: O ye gods,
Render me worthy of this noble wife!
Hark, hark! One knocks. Portia, go in awhile;
And by and by thy bosom shall partake
The secrets of my heart.

At Caesar's house, Caesar's wife, Calphurnia, had been having very bad dreams. Three times in her sleep she called out, "Help, ho! They murder Caesar!"

She and Caesar talked about all the frightening things that had happened in the night. Calphurnia was worried that something very bad was going to happen to Caesar if he went to the Capitol that day. At last, to please Calphurnia, Caesar agreed to stay at home.

CAESAR: Cowards die many times before their deaths;
The valiant never taste of death but once.
Of all the wonders that I yet have heard,
It seems to me most strange that men should fear,
Seeing that death, a necessary end,
Will come when it will come.

Mark Antony came in. Caesar teased him, saying that he had done well to get up after partying all night.

Decius Brutus arrived at Caesar's house. He had to make sure that Caesar went to the Capitol that day.

Caesar told Decius that Calphurnia had had terrible dreams. She had seen Caesar's statue pouring blood, and Romans were smiling, bathing their hands in the blood.

Decius said that was not a bad dream. It showed that Rome got its strength from Caesar.

He made fun of Calphurnia's worries. He told Caesar that the Senate would be offering him a crown that day, to be king of Rome. He said that people would say that Caesar was afraid.

Caesar decided to go.

The other conspirators arrived and Caesar greeted them all as friends.

Caesar was now surrounded by the men who planned to kill him.

In the meantime, a man called Artemidorus had learned of the plot and had made a list of the conspirators. He was going to try to give the list to Caesar.

DECIUS: …Besides, it were a mock
          Apt to be rendered, for someone to say,
          "Break up the Senate till another time,
          When Caesar's wife shall meet with better dreams."
          If Caesar hide himself, shall they not whisper,
          "Lo, Caesar is afraid"?

ACT 3

On the way to the Capitol, Caesar met the soothsayer again. This was the man who had told him to be careful of this very day, the ides of March.

Caesar laughed when he saw him, and said, "The ides of March are come!"

The soothsayer said, "Ay, Caesar, but not gone."

Artemidorus called out, "Hail, Caesar! Read this schedule[1]."

Caesar refused and told him to follow along to the Capitol.

The day hadn't finished. There was plenty of time for things to go wrong for Caesar.

[1]schedule – list.

CAESAR: The ides of March are come.
SOOTHSAYER: Ay, Caesar, but not gone.
ARTEMIDORUS: Hail, Caesar! Read this schedule.

At the Capitol, Caesar was surrounded by people asking him favours. Everyone was talking to him at once.

Metellus Cimber knelt in front of Caesar, asking Caesar to let his brother come back to Rome.

Brutus and Cassius knelt with him, begging Caesar to change his mind.

Casca and Cinna were behind Caesar. When they had Caesar surrounded, Casca gave a signal, "Speak hands for me!"

The conspirators took out their knives and stabbed Caesar. Caesar saw that his friend Brutus was among those stabbing him. He cried, "*Et tu, Brute?*[1] – Then fall Caesar."

[1]*Et tu, Brute?* – Even you, Brutus?

CASCA: Speak hands for me!
CAESAR: *Et tu, Brute?* – Then fall Caesar.

Caesar fell, dead.

Mark Antony came to talk to the conspirators. He said if they were going to kill him too, now was the time to do it. He would die beside Caesar.

Brutus said they did not want to kill him, and he would explain his reasons for killing Caesar. Mark Antony shook hands with the conspirators. He said he would listen to their reasons for thinking that Caesar was so dangerous.

He then asked to speak at Caesar's funeral. Brutus said, "You shall, Mark Antony."

Cassius was not at all happy with the idea. He was afraid that Mark Antony would have a lot of influence with the people. He thought that Brutus had made a bad decision.

Brutus told Mark Antony not to blame them for killing Caesar. He told Mark Antony to say good things about Caesar, and to say that he, Cassius, and the rest, had given him permission to make this speech.

BRUTUS: Mark Antony, here take you Caesar's body.
You shall not in your funeral speech blame us.
But speak all good you can devise of Caesar,
And say you do't by our permission;
Else shall you not have any hand at all
About his funeral.

All the conspirators went away. Mark Antony was left alone with Caesar's body.

He could finally express his real feelings.

He begged Caesar to forgive him for talking to the murderers.

He promised that he would get revenge for Caesar's death.

The servant of Octavius Caesar came in. Young Octavius was an important friend of Caesar. Mark Antony told the servant that Octavius should wait outside the city until it was safe.

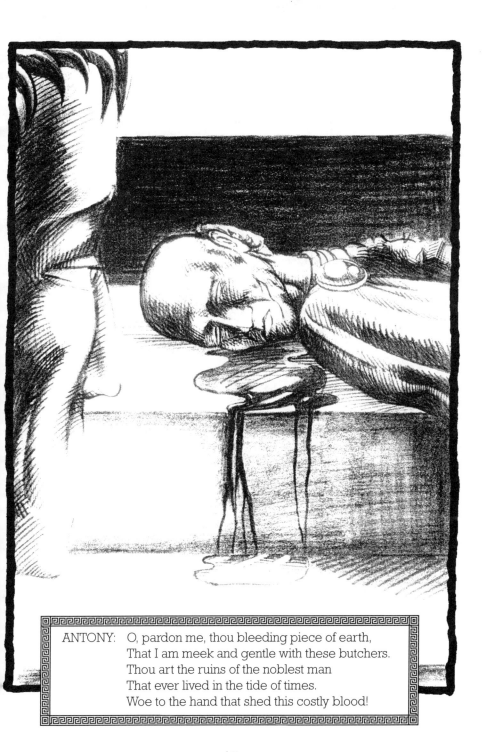

ANTONY: O, pardon me, thou bleeding piece of earth,
         That I am meek and gentle with these butchers.
         Thou art the ruins of the noblest man
         That ever lived in the tide of times.
         Woe to the hand that shed this costly blood!

Julius Caesar

On the day of Caesar's funeral, crowds of people gathered to hear Brutus speak. Brutus stood up and spoke very calmly. He said that he had loved Caesar, but he loved Rome more. He said that if Caesar were alive, Romans would all be his slaves. Now that Caesar was dead, they were all free men.

He talked about Caesar's good qualities.

He said that he had loved Caesar, but hated the fact that Caesar was too ambitious.[1]

He had killed Caesar because of his ambition.

Finally, he said that he, Brutus, was ready to kill himself, if the people wished it.

All the people cheered, and shouted, "Live, Brutus! Live! Live!"

Brutus was very popular at that moment. Some of the people wanted to make him king, now that Caesar was dead.

The people said, "This Caesar was a tyrant[2]." Others said that Rome was lucky to get rid of him.

Brutus told the people that they must now stay and hear what Mark Antony had to say.

---

[1]ambitious – wanting to get ahead; in Caesar's case, greedy for power.
[2]tyrant – a cruel person with a lot of power over people.

BRUTUS: ...If there be any in this assembly, any dear friend of Caesar's, to him I say that Brutus' love to Caesar was no less than his. If then that friend demand why Brutus rose against Caesar, this is my answer: not that I loved Caesar less, but that I loved Rome more.

Julius Caesar

Mark Antony spoke to the people. At first the people did not want to listen to him. He reminded the people of Caesar's good qualities. He tried to show them that Caesar was not ambitious.

Caesar's victories in battle had brought a lot of money to Rome. Caesar had cried for the poor people. When Mark Antony had offered Caesar a crown, to make him king, Caesar refused it three times.

He then pretended to cry, and the people began to feel very sorry about Caesar.

Next, Mark Antony took out Caesar's will. He said he would not read it, because if the people heard it they would be very angry with Brutus and Cassius. Of course, the people shouted to hear the will. They said Mark Antony must read the will.

Mark Antony stepped down, and showed them Caesar's body. He pointed out the stab wounds. Brutus gave the worst blow. That broke Caesar's heart because he had trusted Brutus.

The people became very angry. They started to call the conspirators traitors[1] and villains. They shouted that they wanted to kill the conspirators.

"Revenge! About! Seek! Burn! Fire! Kill! Slay! Let not a traitor live!"

Mark Antony had changed their mood completely.

[1]traitors – people who help to destroy their own country.

ANTONY: Friends, Romans, countrymen, lend me your ears:
I come to bury Caesar, not to praise him.
The evil that men do lives after them,
The good is oft interred with their bones;
So let it be with Caesar.

Mark Antony then read Caesar's will. Caesar had left money and parks to the people of Rome. The people became even more angry.

The crowd had become a mob. The funeral had become a riot.

Mark Antony was very pleased with what he had done.

It was a good time for Octavius Caesar to come back to Rome.

ANTONY: Here is the will, and under Caesar's seal.
To every Roman citizen he gives,
To every several man, seventy-five drachmas.
CROWD: Most noble Caesar! We'll revenge his death!
O royal Caesar!

ACT 4

Three friends of Caesar formed a triumvirate.[1]

The three were Mark Antony, Octavius Caesar, and Lepidus.

They met to plan how they would fight Brutus and Cassius for the control of Rome. First, they decided who had to be killed.

[1]triumvirate – group of three in the place of one leader.
                  Tri means three, as in triangle (three angles)

ANTONY:	These many then shall die; their names are pricked.
OCTAVIUS:	Your brother too must die; consent you, Lepidus?
LEPIDUS:	I do consent.
OCTAVIUS:	Prick him down, Antony.
LEPIDUS:	Upon condition Publius shall not live, Who is your sister's son, Mark Antony.
ANTONY:	He shall not live. Look, with a spot I damn him.

Brutus and Cassius met where they had gathered their armies. They started to argue. Brutus was rude to Cassius, angry and impatient. Cassius had never seen him like this before.

Brutus said that Cassius had taken bribes[1]. He said that Cassius had an itching palm[2].

Cassius became very angry, saying that he was a more experienced soldier than Brutus. Brutus said that he was not afraid of Cassius's anger.

Cassius said that he was afraid he was going to do something he would be sorry for. He might lose his temper and hurt Brutus.

Next, Brutus said that Cassius had refused to send money to pay Brutus's army. Cassius said that the messenger who said that was a fool.

Cassius was very hurt by all the things Brutus had said to him. He offered Brutus his dagger to strike at his heart. Brutus told Cassius to put away the dagger.

[1]bribe – money offered to someone to make him do something dishonest.
[2]an itching palm – a person with an itching palm is holding out his hand hoping for money.

BRUTUS: Let me tell you, Cassius, you yourself
Are much condemned to have an itching palm,
To sell and mart your offices for gold
To undeservers.

CASSIUS: I an itching palm!
You know that you are Brutus that speaks this,
Or, by the gods, this speech were else your last.

Brutus told Cassius that Portia had killed herself. That was the reason he was so upset. Cassius was very sympathetic. He knew that Portia and Brutus had loved each other. He understood why Brutus had seemed so angry.

There was another argument about where the battle with Octavius and Mark Antony should be. Cassius thought they should stay and wait for the enemy. Brutus thought they should march to Philippi before the enemy became more powerful. As usual, Brutus had his own way.

BRUTUS: O Cassius, I am sick of the many griefs.
...Portia is dead.
CASSIUS: Ha? Portia?
BRUTUS: She is dead.
CASSIUS: How scaped I killing when I crossed you so?
O insupportable and touching loss!
Upon what sickness?

That night, Caesar's ghost appeared to Brutus as he tried to sleep. The ghost kept talking about Philippi; he would see Brutus at Philippi. Had Brutus made a wise decision, to fight at Philippi?

BRUTUS: Speak to me what thou art.
GHOST: Thy evil spirit, Brutus.
BRUTUS: Why com'st thou?
GHOST: To tell thee thou shalt see me at Philippi.
BRUTUS: Well; then I shall see thee again?
GHOST: Ay, at Philippi.

ACT 5

Octavius and Mark Antony, Brutus and Cassius, with their armies, met on the battlefield at Philippi.

They spoke angrily to each other.

Cassius reminded Brutus that he had allowed Mark Antony to live and now they were facing his army. Cassius had wanted to kill Mark Antony.

It had been Brutus's decision to let Mark Antony live. It had been Brutus's decision to let him speak at Caesar's funeral, when he changed the mood of the people.

It was Brutus's decision to meet Octavius and Mark Antony at Philippi. How would it turn out?

OCTAVIUS: ...Look,
I draw a sword against conspirators.
When think you that the sword goes up again?
Never till Caesar's three and thirty wounds
Be well avenged; or till another Caesar
Have added slaughter to the sword of traitors.

Cassius and Brutus had a feeling that they might not win the battle. They talked about whether it would be better to be taken prisoner, or to kill themselves. In case they didn't meet again, they said goodbye to each other.

BRUTUS: For ever, and for ever, farewell, Cassius!
If we do meet again, why, we shall smile,
If not, why then this parting was well made.
CASSIUS: For ever, and for ever, farewell, Brutus!
If we do meet again, we'll smile indeed;
If not, 'tis true this parting was well made.

The battle began. Romans were fighting Romans. It was very hard to know which soldiers were friends and which were enemies.

Cassius thought that his friend Titinius was taken prisoner. He thought they were losing the battle.

He asked Pindarus to help him to kill himself. Cassius covered his face and Pindarus killed him with the sword.

CASSIUS: ...Here, take thou the hilt,
And when my face is covered, as 'tis now,
Guide thou the sword. – Caesar, thou art
revenged,
Even with the sword that killed thee.

Titinius and Messala found Cassius's body. Titinius had not been taken prisoner after all, so Cassius had killed himself over a mistake.

Titinius was so upset that he killed himself as well.

Brutus came. Cassius was dead and he had to fight on alone.

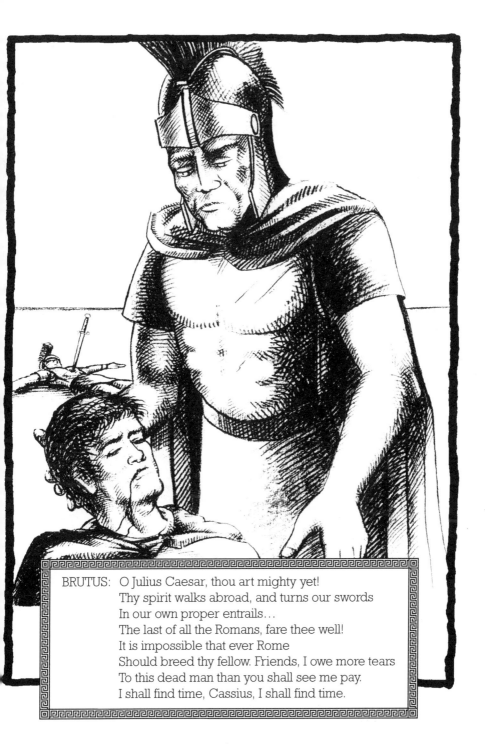

BRUTUS: O Julius Caesar, thou art mighty yet!
Thy spirit walks abroad, and turns our swords
In our own proper entrails...
The last of all the Romans, fare thee well!
It is impossible that ever Rome
Should breed thy fellow. Friends, I owe more tears
To this dead man than you shall see me pay.
I shall find time, Cassius, I shall find time.

Brutus realised that the battle was lost. He asked his soldiers, one by one, to help him kill himself. He did not want to be taken prisoner by Mark Antony and Octavius.

Brutus's soldiers did not want to help him kill himself. Finally, Strato agreed. He held the sword and Brutus ran upon it.

Brutus died at Philippi. It had been another bad decision.

Mark Antony and Octavius found Brutus's body.

Mark Antony said, "This was the noblest Roman of them all."

BRUTUS: Night hangs upon mine eyes; my bones would rest,
That have but laboured to attain this hour…
Farewell, good Strato. – Caesar, now be still;
I killed not thee with half so good a will.